A Kid's Guide to Managing Money

A Children's Book about Money Management

by

Joy Wilt

Illustrated by Ernie Hergenroeder

 CHILDRENS PRESS, CHICAGO

Author

JOY WILT is creator and director of Children's Ministries, an organization that provides resources "for people who care about children"—speakers, workshops, demonstrations, consulting services, and training institutes. A certified elementary school teacher, administrator, and early childhood specialist, Joy is also consultant to and professor in the master's degree program in children's ministries for Fuller Theological Seminary. Joy is a graduate of LaVerne College, LaVerne, California (B.A. in Biological Science), and Pacific Oaks College, Pasadena, California (M.A. in Human Development). She is author of three books, *Happily Ever After, An Uncomplicated Guide to Becoming a Superparent*, and *Taming the Big Bad Wolves*, as well as the popular *Can-Make-And-Do Books*. Joy's commitment "never to forget what it feels like to be a child" permeates the many innovative programs she has developed and her work as lecturer, consultant, writer, and—not least—mother of two children, Christopher and Lisa.

Artist

ERNIE HERGENROEDER is founder and owner of Hergie & Associates (a visual communications studio and advertising agency). With the establishment of this company in 1975, "Hergie" and his wife, Faith, settled in San Jose with their four children, Lynn, Kathy, Stephen, and Beth. Active in community and church affairs, Hergie is involved in presenting creative workshops for teachers, ministers, and others who wish to understand the techniques of communicating visually. He also lectures in high schools to encourage young artists toward a career in commercial art. Hergie serves as a consultant to organizations such as the Police Athletic League (PAL), Girl Scouts, and religious and secular corporations. His ultimate goal is to touch the hearts of kids (8 to 80) all over the world—visually!

Library of Congress Cataloging in Publication Data

Wilt, Joy.
   A kid's guide to managing money.

   1.   Finance, Personal—Juvenile literature.
2.   Money—Juvenile literature.   I.   Hergenroeder, Ernie.   II.   Title.
HG179.W539   1982   332.024'054   81-21768
ISBN 0-516-02512-0   AACR2

1982 CHILDRENS PRESS EDITION

Contents

Introduction

A Kid's Guide to Managing Money is designed to involve the reader in the concepts that are being taught. This is done by simply and carefully explaining each concept and then asking questions that invite a response from the reader. It is hoped that by answering the questions the reader will personalize the concept and, thus, integrate it into his or her thinking.

A Kid's Guide to Managing Money explains where money came from and why it exists today. Readers are given creative money-making projects to help them "make" money. Once money has been earned, it must be managed. Guidelines for saving, donating, and spending money are given.

A Kid's Guide to Managing Money is designed to teach children that money when gotten fairly and used properly can be a wonderful thing. This book is also designed to teach a child that learning to "make and manage money" is a part of becoming an adult. People who grow up believing and accepting this will be better equipped to live healthy, exciting lives.

A Kid's Guide to Managing Money

If you have money or would like to have money, this book is for you.

9

No matter who you are . . .

money is a part of your life.

11

But what is money?

Where did it come from?

Chapter 1

How Money Began

A long time ago, money wasn't needed because each family worked to supply the things it used. The family members made their own clothing, built their own shelter, and . . .

grew and hunted their own food.

15

But then people began to realize that no one person or family could do everything.

They realized that some people were good at doing some things
while other people were good at other things.

So people decided to trade the things they owned for other things.

This was called bartering.

At one time, animals like cows, pigs, and sheep were popular trading items because they provided meat, milk, and leather hides.

But because all animals were not equal in value, trading animals presented problems. People needed something that could be divided so they could trade a fair and equal amount when they bartered.

21

People also needed something that was easy to carry.

They needed something that didn't require care
and that could be easily stored.

23

This is where grain and salt came into the picture.

Beads, shells, tea, tobacco, fish hooks, rubber, animal teeth, claws, feathers, and furs also became popular items for people to barter with.

People also used metal to barter with. Jewelry, pots, tools, and weapons — all made of copper, lead, gold, silver, and tin were among the many metal trading items.

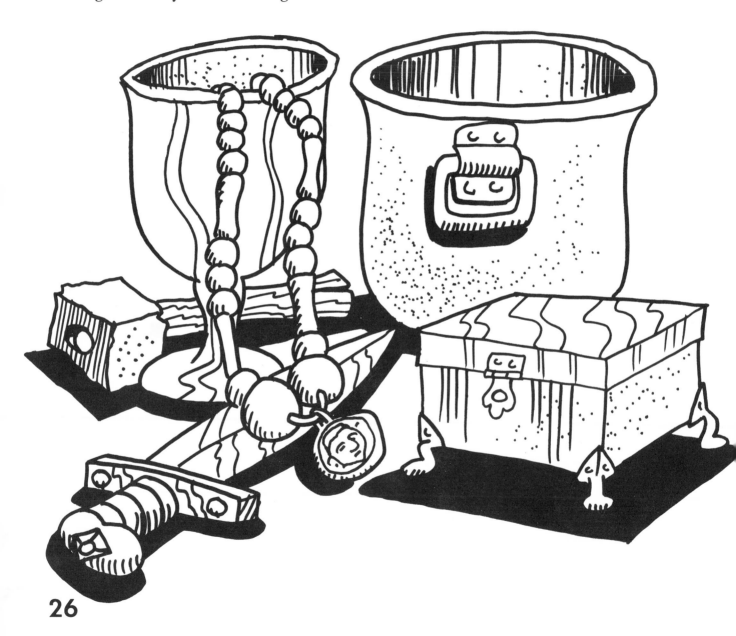

In time, people decided that metal, especially gold and
silver, was the best thing to barter with.

So these metals were formed into coins. According to their size and weight, metal coins were worth different amounts. These coins were easily recognized, kept their value, and were small enough to be carried.

But metal coins were heavy and hard to handle if a person had very many of them. People needed something lightweight to make trading easier.

29

So paper money began to be used, first in China, then across the world.

Paper money was a promise to pay metal coins in the amount printed on the paper. These paper notes could be exchanged for the valuable metal coins.

Today in America, both metal coins and paper money are used to barter with.

Can you name the coins and paper money on these two pages?

Why do you need money?

Chapter 2

Needing Money

Money can make it possible for you to buy some of the things you need.

Money can make it possible for you to buy some of the things you want.

37

Money can help make some of your dreams come true.

Money can help you do some of the things you want to do.

Money can help you show love and appreciation to other people.

Money can make it possible for you to help other people.

Money can help you get in control of your life.

Money can help you be your own boss.

43

How can you get money?

Chapter 3

Getting Money

There are several ways you can get money.

You may get an allowance. This allowance is probably a set amount of money given to you by your parents once a day or once every week. Some children are given allowances without any work expected in return. Other children may have to do small chores or jobs to earn their allowances.

Sometime you might find money that another person has lost. If this happens, you should try to find the owner and return the money. If you can't find the owner, then the money is yours to keep.

At special times, you may receive money from someone as a gift.

HAPPY BIRTHDAY, STEVE!

An allowance is great, finding money is exciting, and receiving money as a gift is fun. However, you may not want to count on these three things to supply enough money for you.

There are at least two more ways to get money.

You can sell something to someone . . .

HEY, HOW WOULD YOU LIKE TO BUY MY SKATES? THEY ARE TOO SMALL FOR MY FEET NOW, BUT THEY LOOK LIKE THEY MIGHT FIT YOU PERFECTLY!

or do something for someone and charge him or her for your services.

If you decide to sell something to someone, you could choose to sell something you already own. It is a good idea to get an OK from your parents before you sell anything. Here is a list of things you might own and would want to sell.

Old toys, games, or sports equipment.

Outgrown clothes.

Used Halloween costumes.

Old records or recorded tapes.

Old magazines, reading books, or comic books.

Outgrown tricycles, bicycles, or scooters.

Pets or babies of those pets.

BABY RABBITS FOR SALE

You could choose to sell something you have collected. Here is a list of possible things to collect for sale.

Old newspapers or aluminum cans for sale to be recycled.

Seashells, starfish, and sand dollars.

Rocks and minerals.

Decorative tree bark, twigs, branches, seeds, pods, pinecones, mistletoe, dry weeds, and flowers.

Product coupons from newspapers, magazines, cereal boxes, and advertising mailings.

Glass bottles which can be returned to the store for a refund, recycled, or sold for other uses.

Fresh flowers.

"Good" junk and reusable discards.

Fresh fruit, vegetables, and herbs.

Collectable postage stamps and coins.

Old clothes for Halloween costumes or playing dress up.

You could choose to sell something you have made. Here is a list of possible things to make for sale.

Ice cold drinks like lemonade, orange juice, grape juice, punch, or other fruit juice drinks.

Homemade cakes, cookies, candies, or other baked food items.

Sandwiches.

Ice cream sundaes, sodas, Popsicles, or other sweet treats.

Pot holders, aprons, or tie-dyed tee shirts, scarves, or clothing patches.

Decorated boxes.

Macrame art pieces.

Puppets.

Bird feeders or houses.

Clay pottery.

Leather craft work.

Candles.

Beanbags.

Patchwork cloth items.

Dried or pressed flowers.

Drawstring bags.

Green plants started from seeds or cuttings.

Terrariums.

Handmade greeting cards and stationery.

You could choose to sell something on a consignment plan. Consignment means to give over to another person's care. Here's how the plan works.

Step 1 — Find someone who wants to sell something he or she owns. Agree upon an amount of money the owner wants to sell the object for and an amount of money you should get from the owner for finding a buyer for the object.

Step 2 — Take the object that needs to be sold and find someone else who wants to buy it.

Step 3 — If you sell the object, take the money to the first owner and ask for the money you should get for the job of selling the object.

Step 4 — If you don't sell the object, you should take the object back to the the owner without cost to you.

A yard or garage sale is a very good way to sell things using the consignment plan.

59

You may not choose to sell something to get money because you might prefer to do something for someone else and get paid for your services.

PUTT
PUTT

If you like to do indoor jobs, then here is a list of possible ways to earn money.

Make and pack sack lunches for your family.

Clean and polish shoes.

Water and care for your parents' houseplants.

Prepare a meal for your family and clean up afterward.

Clean and wax furniture.

Help with regular house cleaning chores or thorough " spring-cleaning" jobs.

Sew on buttons and mend clothing that needs fixing.

Clean up before, during, and after parties.

Polish metal household items like silver dinnerware or brass door handles.

Care for a family's house while they are on vacation. You might offer to water indoor plants, feed their pets, turn their lights on at night, or collect their newspapers and mail.

Ask a local store manager if he or she needs anyone to help straighten and clean up.

63

If you like to do outdoor jobs, then here is a list of possible ways you can earn money.

Walk other people's dogs.

Weed flower beds and gardens.

Rake leaves.

Mow lawns.

Clean animal cages, pens, houses, and stables.

Paint house numbers on the street curbs in front of people's houses.

Paint outdoor lawn furniture.

Shovel paths, sidewalks, and driveways after it snows in winter.

Sweep the street pavement on your block and ask each neighbor to give a little toward the total price of the job.

Offer a local store manager your services to run errands and make deliveries.

Brush, clean, and vacuum the insides of cars.

Scrub and wash the outsides of cars.

Start an errand running service and offer to run errands at any time.

SNIFF

65

If you like working with younger children, then here is a list of possible ways to earn money. It would be best if you got permission from your parents and the children's parents before you set out to do these jobs.

Take a baby for a stroller or baby carriage ride.

Watch a toddler while he or she plays in a water sprinkler or wading pool.

Take a child to a park to play.

Help parents plan and put on a birthday party for their child.

Take a child to the library and help him or her choose books and return them on time.

Walk with a young child to and from school.

Keep a child busy and entertained while his or her parents rest or do other things.

If you like working with older adults, then here is a list of possible ways to earn money.

Take an older person on regular walks.

Help with housecleaning jobs.

Read newspapers, magazines, books, letters, and other mail out loud.

Write letters and cards for an older person.

Do grocery shopping or other marketing.

Run errands and make deliveries such as taking mail to and from the post office.

Help an older person keep up his or her lawn, garden, or house work and repairs.

Prepare meals and clean up afterward.

If you like to entertain or perform for people, then here is a list of possible ways to earn money. Invite your family, relatives, friends, and neighbors to these entertainment events and charge an admission fee.

Hold a "story hour" reading for younger children.

Produce a variety show.

Perform a play or puppet show.

Put on a "dress up" fashion show.

Present a magic show with tricks you have made.

Develop a professional looking clown, monster, or movie star costume and make appearances at birthday parties or other special events.

PUPPET
SHOW
TODAY

71

If you like to do things that are somewhat "out of the ordinary," then here is a list of possible ways to earn money.

Start a rental service and rent your toys, games, and sports equipment to anyone who will take care of them.

Produce a neighborhood newspaper which includes neighborhood news, announcements, want ads, cartoons, and riddles and jokes. Sell the newspapers door to door to the people in the neighborhood.

Use a camera to take pictures of people at home, church, school, or anywhere around the neighborhood. Sell the pictures you make to the people you've photographed or their families. It is good to know that parents are always interested in having pictures of their children.

Start a pet cleaning and grooming service.

Write and draw pictures to illustrate a book about the people you know. Include interesting things about people in your family, school, and neighborhood. Make copies of the book and sell them. It is good to know that people who are included in the book will probably want to buy copies.

Repair and service tricycles and bicycles.

Open a gift wrapping service and decorate packages for
birthdays, weddings, Christmas and other holiday seasons.

Pick a school subject that you do well in and tutor children
who have problems with that subject.

Put on a pet show, a hobby display, or an arts and crafts fair
and charge an admission price to see the show. Participants
in the show should receive paper certificate or ribbon awards.

Umpire or referee at neighborhood sports games.

Make a spook house and charge a fee to go through it.

But whether you sell something...

you already own,
you have collected,
you have made, or
on consignment plan,

or whether you work...

    indoors,

    outdoors,

    with younger children,

    with older adults,

    on a performance,

    or do things out of the ordinary,

there are eight things you must do to make sure your efforts make money.

Step one is to decide what you would like to do to earn money.

As you decide, consider these three things.

What do you enjoy doing?

What can you do well?

What goods or services do the people around you want?

If you plan to make money by selling to or working for your family, relatives, friends, and neighbors, then you need to find out what they want or need.

 Three good ways you can use to find out are . . .

Look around and see if you can discover things that people might want or things that need to be done.

Talk with people either in person or by telephone.

Hand out a sheet of questions with a place for people to say what they need or want. This is called a questionnaire.

Here is a sample.

PLEASE FILL OUT THIS QUESTIONNAIRE AND RETURN IT TO STEVE. Thank you

PLACE A **NUMBER** IN EACH BLANK TO SHOW HOW MANY TIMES YOU WOULD USE OR WANT THESE GOODS AND SERVICES IN OUR NEIGHBORHOOD.

PUT $\frac{1}{2}$ FOR ONCE A WEEK, OR $\underline{3}$ FOR LESS **OFTEN**, FOR ONCE A **MONTH**,

—— RENTING AND REPAIRING SERVICE FOR TOY AND PLAY EQUIPMENT.
—— CUSTOM-MADE MACRAME HANGINGS.
—— NEIGHBORHOOD ERRAND AND DELIVERY SERVICE.
—— PET-CARE SERVICE FOR FEEDING, WALKING, CLEANING, AND GROOMING.

WHAT OTHER SERVICES AND GOODS WOULD YOU LIKE TO HAVE? ____
_____
_____
_____

Step two is to do research.

You should find out these three things.

How can you do what you would like to do?
How much will your project cost you?
How much time will your project take to do?

You can answer these questions by doing research at the library and getting information and advice from other people.

79

Step three is to get permission from your family to do what you want to do.

Make sure that your money-making project will not cause problems for your parents or other family members.

81

Step four is to learn how to do what you have decided to do.

If you plan to make something to sell, learn how to make it so that people will want to buy it.

If you plan to do something for someone and charge for your services, learn how to do your job so that people will want to hire you.

You can learn a skill by studying library books or having someone teach you how.

Step five is to decide on a fair price for your product or service.

As you decide, consider these three things.

How much will the project cost you?

How much time will the project take to do?

How much will people be willing to pay for your
product or service?

If you charge too much, you may not be able to sell your product or service. If you charge too little, then you will probably lose the time and money you put into the project. You may want to ask an adult to help you set fair prices.

Step six is to let people know about your product or service.

This is called advertising. Here are some good ways you can advertise.

Place information about your product or service in the local newspaper.

Put notices on bulletin boards in community centers, local stores, laundromats, or any place where people will see them.

Make signs to put in front of your house and in other good spots.

List important information about your product or service on a sheet of paper. Print copies of this paper or flier and then hand them out to the neighborhood people.

Step seven is to sell your product or service.

The best way is for you to begin talking with people in person or on the telephone.

If you have enough money, you might choose to pay someone else to help you sell your product or service.

Step eight is to deliver your product or service.

You should always keep these four things in mind.

Make sure you deliver your product or service on time.
Make sure you deliver everything you promised to deliver.
Make sure everything you sell is in good condition.
Make sure you do your best at every job.

91

Here again are the eight things you must do to make sure you make money.

Decide what you would like to do to earn money.

Do research.

Get permission from your family to do what you want to do.

Learn how to do what you have decided to do.

Decide on a fair price for your product or service.

Let people know about your product or service.

Sell your product or service.

Deliver your product or service.

After you have made money, what will you do with it?

Chapter 4

Using Money

There are three main things you can do with money.

You can save money.

You can give money away.

You can spend money.

It is very wise for you to do all three things with your money.

You should learn to . . .

     save some money,
     give some money away, and
     spend some money.

Saving money means storing or putting it away for later use. It is a good idea to save at least ten percent of your money. You can save your money at home by placing it in a container and then putting the container away in a safe place.

101

Another way you can save your money is by letting a bank keep your money for you. This is done by placing your money in a savings account.

Putting your money in a bank is a good idea because money is safer there and is less likely to get lost or stolen.

103

If saving your money at a bank sounds like a good idea, then you should go to a bank and talk to the person in charge of starting new savings accounts.

104

GIVING YOUR MONEY AWAY

Giving money away usually means giving to groups
of people or organizations that help other people.
These organizations are usually nonprofit. This
means they are not in business to make money.
These groups work with money that is given or
donated to them to help others.

The Red Cross,

Goodwill Industries,

the Salvation Army,

Boy Scouts of America,

the Girl Scouts of the United States of America, and
your church

. . . are just a few of the nonprofit organizations that
accept donations and use the money to help people.

Nonprofit organizations help people.

Your donation will be used to make it possible for the
nonprofit organization to inspire, educate, and help
other people.

107

Your donation will be used to help many people.

SPENDING YOUR MONEY

In addition to saving and giving away money, spending is another way you can use money.

It is important for you to learn how to spend your money wisely. There are several things that are good to do before spending your money.

The first thing you should do before you spend any money is plan how you are going to use your money. This plan of how you want to use your money is called a budget.

A budget should list your income and your expenses.

Income means how much money you have and
    where it came from.

Expenses means how you plan to use your money.
    Expenses would include some or all of the following
    list.

        Savings or how much money you plan to save.

        Donations or how much money you plan to give
            away including your tithe.

        Needs or what things you need to buy.

        Wants or what things you would like to buy.

Here is a sample budget sheet which should help you plan your use of money.

THIS IS MY BUDGET FOR THE WEEK OF: _____
DATE

MY INCOME:

    ALLOWANCE $ _____
    WORK EARNINGS $ _____
    OTHER $ _____

        TOTAL INCOME $ _____

MY EXPENSES:

    SAVINGS $ _____
    DONATIONS $ _____
    NEEDS $ _____
    WANTS $ _____

        TOTAL EXPENSES $ _____

If your total expenses add up to more than your total income, then you're in trouble. You can't spend more money than you have.

When your total expenses are more than your total income, you can do one of two things. You can either make more money to add to your income . . .

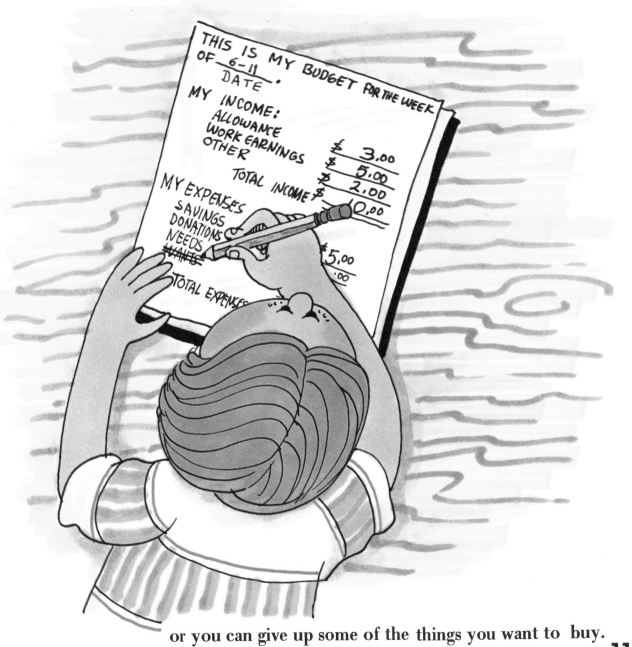

or you can give up some of the things you want to buy.

The second thing you should do before you spend any money is to list the things you need and want in order from the most important to the least important. Such a list is often called a priority list.

To make a priority list, make a list of everything you need or want. Next, make another list; only this time place the most important things at the top of the list and the least important things at the bottom. Then you should always try to buy things in the order they are on your list.

The third thing you should do before you spend any money is think about what you are buying before you buy it.

I'D BETTER NOT BUY THIS NOW BECAUSE THEN I WOULDN'T HAVE ENOUGH MONEY FOR MY LUNCH.

Buy things that do what they are supposed to do. Make
sure that they really work.

Buy things that are not already damaged or broken.

Make sure the things you buy are made well and are sturdy enough not to be easily damaged or broken.

Buy things that are safe. Do not buy things that could hurt you or someone else.

Make sure you pay a fair price for the things you buy. This may mean that you should check prices in several stores before you buy what you want.

Buy things from a store that can be respected and has a good reputation. A good store will always take responsibility for the things sold to you.

If you have any doubts or questions about something you are going to buy, talk to your parents before you buy the item.

Remember these things.

Plan a budget for your money,

Make a priority list of the things you need
or want to buy, and

Think before you buy something.

If you do these things, you will find that the money you have worked hard to get will add to your life because . . .

Money, when gotten fairly and used in a good way . . .

can be a wonderful thing!